passages

Also by jenni nixon and published by Ginninderra Press
swimming underground

jenni nixon

passages

GP

Acknowledgements

thanks to editors who published earlier versions of poems
harbour city poets   voices from underground
ginninderra press   rochford street review
not very quiet   cordite   southerly
spineless wonders   old water rat publishing   burrow
kistrech kenya   world anthologies   meuse press
for ukraine by women of the world   aclw.org

sincere thanks
stephen matthews oam
sara dowse
don maynard
roundtable writing group
friends who kept me safe during pandemic
ancestry.com

broadcast poems with gayle austin   curved radio 2ser
shortlisted joanne burns award   pulped fiction

passages was written while on land of the gadigal people

passages
ISBN 978 1 76109 431 6

Cover image: *sailing*, acrylic on canvas, by the author

First published 2022 by
GINNINDERRA PRESS
PO Box 3461 Port Adelaide 5015
www.ginninderrapress.com.au

Contents

'you're living for nothing now
i hope you're keeping some kind of record'
– leonard cohen, 'famous blue raincoat'

'we must admit there will be music despite everything'
– rebecca solnit

1

arrival and departures

thomas and jane rose

18/01/1788   eleven tall ships sail into *sydney cove*
  gadigal[1] men wade out to greet them
anchor drops at *warrang*[2] after seven month journey
crew   civilians   marines   convicts all disembark
  (twelve men were of *african* descent[3])
  'here they raise *british* flag   claim land   toast the king
  look warily into surrounding bush'[4]   no treaty
betray indigenous who inhabit country sixty thousand years
  eora people of gadigal nation are curious but suspicious
colony later sail to *port jackson*   sheltered   fresh water
'a thousand sail of the line in the most perfect security'[5]
(introduced species   cattle   horse   sheep   swine   rabbits)
within ten years most local *indigenous* people are dead
  devastated by smallpox   shot or poisoned
convict life harsh in canvas tents and makeshift shelters
drunken castaways   women raped   men lashed or hanged
'damned whores they say the cause of much dissension'[6]
livestock die of disease or wander off   struck by lightning
second fleet (*death fleet*) a disaster   dead   dying men stink
leg irons expose bone   ulcerated sores seep pus
  ravaged by sickness   up to ten a day die upon arrival
illness in colony has it close to starvation and failure
  fresh water hauled from rock pools dug in tank stream
birds and seafood plundered   food provisions improve
'the pot received everything we could catch or kill'[7]
  prison camp turning into *ye olde english town*

convicts upon sentence served may receive land
   more if married   build cottages with gardens
workshops   timberyards   brick kilns
   'plan hospital   jail   court and church'[8]
babies born   some are of *aboriginal* blood
england's stately homes aristocracy grows plump
   fruit of largest empire in history
ladies dance lift leg with flounce and turn
lords shoot grouse on green moors destitute starve
sentenced to death or given transportation for life
often minor crimes   theft of food or livestock
left old warships and merchant vessels
   prison hulks   moored on *river thames*
screams shatter quiet mornings   startle swans
temporary measure that lasts for eighty years

governor phillip's frequent requests to *admiralty*
   dispatch experienced farmers:
'if fifty farmers were sent out with their families[9]
they would do more in one year in rendering
this colony independent of the *mother country*
as to provisions than a thousand convicts
the right kind of settler be given free passage
land grant   tools   two year's provisions
one year service of convict labour'[10]

they hang the man and flog the woman
that steal the goose from off the common,
but let the greater villain loose
that steals the common from the goose.

the law demands that we atone
when we take things we do not own
but leaves the lords and ladies fine
who take things that are yours and mine.

the poor and wretched don't escape
if they conspire the law to break;
this must be so but they endure
those who conspire to make the law.

the law locks up the man or woman
who steals the goose from off the common
and geese will still a common lack
till they go and steal it back.

(17th-century nursery rhyme, anonymous)

puxey farm in *sturminster newton*   *dorset*
thomas and jane rose (4th great-grandparents)
leave farm with four children   niece and milkmaid
choose five month voyage to other side of the world
on small property were too many mouths to feed
(thomas rose: 'most respectable of these people
apparently best calculated for a bona-fide settler'[11])
perilous stagecoach journey fear what lies ahead
strange 'new' land   never to see home again
   settlers reach *gravesend*   jostled by crowds
hands tucked into warm mittens   petticoats rustle
bewigged gentlemen   woollen country folk hustle
farmers who lost common land   'middling class'
bustle among hubbub of pickpockets   'foreign' pimps
prostitutes   flash confidence men and mudlarkers
   ignore warnings of dangerous mud
   'might right there swallow you 'ole'
settlers stop at an old inn   hear stories to curdle your blood
held nearby in dark cells women prisoners moan
curse their fate   supply ship   *bellona*
with civilian and military crew set sail from *gravesend*
squashed in cramped quarters five settler families
farmers   fisherman   baker   blacksmith and female convicts
three thousand pounds of tobacco   port wine   rum   molasses
pork   cloth and paper   in heavy seas on five-month journey
supplies ruined by storm damage   stink   rotten and maggoty

free settler or felon   sick with scurvy
   worm fever and convulsions
marooned for days on blue-green sea
bobbing beneath canopy of stars
dairymaid escapes smell of sickness
unwashed people and sweaty fear
packed together like fish in fishmonger's basket
   briefly allowed up on deck to dream
she's pulling pink udders   cow eyes flooding tears
sailor who gifts her posy of field flowers
   woken by sudden movement she feels
breeze take hold in sheet-flapping sails
an albatross swoops   glide on airflows   flies ahead

jane rose darns petticoat torn on wooden decking
   sews criss-cross stars of milky way into garment
smiles at ocean as if big waves were friends
niece elizabeth sniffs in hope that journey
fill with promise   day's heat be pleasant not unbearable
ship heaves side to side   among disgusting smells
   jane calmly nurses son richard sick with convulsions
'this is not what i signed up for' pregnant elizabeth fish
aged eighteen cries 'will edward still ask for my hand?'
   baby lost to fever before voyage ends

bellona 16th january 1793 arrive in *new south wales*
thomas and jane rose thomas jnr thirteen mary eleven
joshua nine richard three years settle at *hunter's hut*
liberty plains (*homebush*) on land grant of poor soil
no manure inadequate water *english* crops wither and die
'hasty and bad choice of situation'[12] they move to *prospect*

pemulwuy of *bidigal* clan led fighters and escaped convicts
'in war of resistance burning crops and attacking farmers'[13]
dusk message sticks clack shadows glimmer in *corroboree*[14]
settlers with aching homesickness isolation and illness
fear warring natives slithering snakes animals who hop
spiders kookaburras' wild cackles of laughter at dawn
lorikeets squawk-screech in rapid burst of harsh sunlight
cloudless blue skies that stretch to endless horizons
no sweet *english* wren's chirrup on green fields of home

letter dated 10 march 1798 sent by thomas and mary topp
from *sturminster* to their daughter jane and son-in-law
thomas rose: 'the times in *england* are verey hasardous
and eavery thing is very dear and eavery week threttn'd with
a invasion by the *french* and wee believe it will shurely be so
as they are fully intended to invade this cuntry the taxes heare
hardly to be borne they are so heavy a tax opon saddle horses
three guineas a year a hard tax pon dogs they talk pon
taxing cows and many other taxes too tedious to mention.'[15]

thomas rose   overseer in charge government farm and stock
had twin sons   john and henry   six months upon arrival
1795 sarah   '*first free settler*' children born in colony
granted land   seven years of crop failures   water shortages
no prospect there   too hard to hoe rock and dry dirt
   purchase thirty acres of more fertile land
on the move again to *wilberforce*   country of *dharug* people
away from flood plains near *hawkesbury river*[16] (*dyarubbin*)[17]
builds house   begun in 1811   timber slab with split rafters
two brick chimneys   *rose cottage* heritage-listed
   oldest extant slab timber cottage in *australia*

thomas and jane married forty-eight years   had eleven children
   not all survived

rose cottage[18] 2020

sarah ann rose (1795–1869) at *rose cottage*
  studies her mother jane rose seated on veranda:
'whalebone stays stopped spear thrown by native
saved her   though why i wonder in all this heat
  why does mother still bother wearing them?
she sits on veranda sewing abandoned on her lap
gazes at sunlight pattern leaves with flakes of gold
fires were burning   men helped put them out
blackened trees scar our landscape grey smoke
hangs thick while all around there's commotion
older brother's boots thump floor importantly
helping father build slab shed out to side of cottage
shout to each other as if one's here
  other way up on top paddock
1803   joshua and henry had returned to *england* to fight
part-time soldiers against napoleon if he were to invade
two years training   they thought were going for a lark
were no invasion   so back they come to us here at home
youngest brother spins metal top brought from *england*
colours whizz round fast in speedy blur like memories
fear of drunken men on rum worry about night noises
animals that crash through bush   branches crack
  escaped convict or natives come for food?
  we give 'em bread   send on way
don't have much but mother says ours a christian home'

'…notwithstanding their having been frequently called upon and admonished to discontinue their hostile incursions and treated on all these occasions with the greatest kindness and forbearance by government… having nevertheless recently committed several cruel and most barbarous murders on the settlers and their families and servants, killed their cattle, and robbed them of their grain and other property to a considerable amount, it becomes absolutely necessary to put a stop to these outrages and disturbances, and to adopt the strongest and most coercive measures to prevent a recurrence of them…all *aborigines* from *sydney* onwards are to be made prisoners of war and if they resist they are to be shot and their bodies hung from trees in the most conspicuous places near where they fall, so as to strike terror into the hearts of surviving natives.'

– governor lachlan macquarie 1816
diary & memorandum book[19]

henry buttsworth aka bozeat or boswaite in 1810
stands in dock of *northampton assizes*[20]
'charged with stealing four ewe sheep property of w. smith'
meanwhile hundred guests in nearby banquet hall spoon
green turtle soup   each bowl scullery maid's yearly wage
(now endangered with overharvesting loss of nesting sites)
  henry receives 'sentence of death but were reprieved'
transported for term of his life aged twenty-two
one of two hundred convicts on the *guildford*
arrives in 1812 year later marries sarah ann rose
  st matthews anglican church at *windsor*
designed by francis greenway and built by convicts
  still serving his sentence   released into her custody
at *wilberforce*   freeperson   farmer   grew wheat / maize
founds a mill   given pardon gains one hundred fifteen acres
builds large two-storey brick home   had seven children
six horses sixty-seven horned cattle   one hundred sixty sheep
  1840   older brother william   aged fifty-one
charged with receiving stolen sheep
sentenced to fifteen years arrives *sydney cove* on the *eden*
married with six children   could neither read or write
  after ten years given ticket-of-leave
worked as shepherd   upon serving out sentence
returned home to *england*   did brothers ever meet
before paths went their separate ways?

3rd great-grandfather robert james nixon
born 1803 *england*   seaman on convict ship *heroine*
died *windsor* 1875   son james robert nixon
  born *london* 1831   in *pitt town hawkesbury* district
1854 marries granddaughter of thomas and jane rose
  sarah ann buttsworth had nine children
story within the family goes they are *anglican*
until one day james robert heard loud noises
a rider who flogs   curses horse that gallops to and fro
whinnying in agitation   visiting parson
  worse for wear in liquor so disgusts
james robert that he becomes *wesleyan*
later family have strong association
  with *temperance movement*[21]

sarah ann nixon sits between two daughters
eliza and alice   long black frock scalloped at hem
holds posy of flowers stares grim-faced   stern
  pose in black and white photograph
as if sitting modern passport photo   unsmiling
  way photos were back then

2nd great-grandfather james robert dies aged 53
buried at *willow point cemetery*
  long neglected   difficult to acccss
occupies overgrown site near river east of *nabiac*

james henry nixon (great grandfather)   grazier
1859   born *windsor*   married margaret hawkins 1885
had five children   dies in 1940   resident of *nabiac*
his son john garfield nixon (paternal grandfather 1887–1965)
married elizabeth mary croker   1887–1936   (grandmother)
she had thirteen siblings   five children   died aged forty-nine
he married again   mollie noble had son   two daughters
aged 78   he died at *gloucester* nsw and is buried there

stayed at *bundook* for a year   chaos at home
went to one-room school with young relatives
granddad sat with shotgun   keeping fruit bats at bay
log fire in kitchen stove crackled and spat
sometimes he tickled favourite cat
gnarled fingers stretched hind legs 'high flyer'
jumped hurdles over strong tanned hands
had largest bible had ever seen   family history
in different inscriptions   generations scribbled on title page
dawdled   poked baked cowpats with stick
helped bring in poddies   beautiful soft mouth young cows
tapped knuckles on water tank for level
played 'snap' on veranda   coloured ribbons tacked to wall
  champion bulls and heifers that trod winners' circle
royal easter show   granddad died   grazing lands sold
  maybe too hard plant more dreams

rose cottage 2/02/2020

bushfires burnt for months   lives and properties lost
outside heat is intense   which way do we go?
gouged-out freeways confuse   travel through *windsor*
historic *governor macquarie* town
bitter battle fought to save 1874 bridge
new three-lane bridge forges toward *wilberforce*
goes under in flooding that followed fires
watered turf grown green on flat flood plains
we cross *buttsworth creek* that flows into *hawkesbury river*
henry buttsworth established his steam-mill nearby
disappointment awaits us   cottage enclosed by chain fence
   rose cottage closed   locked   had appointment just too hot
wedding party arrives at *pioneer village* nearby
we're allowed in on quick visit to wander and photograph
imagine thomas and jane seated on veranda
seated this very spot   travelled such long distance
doors have no knob or keyholes   cottage holds its secrets
   bigger on inside than out like the *tardis*?
more questions than answers is there a creek nearby?
   what is history of local *dharug* people?
   replaced renovated cladding too neat
old timbers peek from under eaves   glimpse builder's skills
   what did rickety timber slab shed hold?   we hurry out
retreat back to *windsor* to *crepe escape* for lunch

2

another voyage

george and selina kershaw

george kershaw – 1801–1878
selina kershaw (née hirst) – 1802--1855
3rd great-grandparents
5/12/1841 arrive in colony on board *columbine*

sydney is an old tart forever under the knife
dug up and rebuilt tunnelled out again
flashy toothless smile for all to see
at *mitchell library*
seated among stored memories
permitted to touch without gloves
slim brown leather diary
in fine ink penmanship
'george kershaw schoolmaster'
pages covered in numbers with timeline

george – august 1841
at anchor in *victoria dock liverpool*
taken in tow by steam tug set sail
'bound for *sidney* gave them three hearty cheers'
two hundred forty emigrants 'not all sick'[22]
includes son william five matilda three emma a year
rough night wet 'wind boisterous
lost seaman overbord and drownded
four seamen went in got his cap'
fine weather enter *bay of biscay*
'wife better and children well sea calm'

george – september
appointed schoolmaster for ship
'droves of porpoises nearly all well on bord
had prayers   sung for first time
mrs brown confined to childbed of a son
very raining all day no prayers
ships pass   sometimes speak'
ship from *batavia* bound to *amsterdam*
'spoke *the mary* the other side *the cape*
bound to *calcutta* with troops'
see whale ship burning oil he thought on fire

selina – september
1823 married george kershaw in *leeds yorkshire*
selina below deck in chilly damp quarters
'ship creaking fit to shake off timber bones
keep her afloat   william allowed up
during light rain see men take in sails
women kept confined when storms rage
emma screams for milk but sad there's none
cannot afford wet-nurse'   (thirteen pregnancies
seven buried in one grave at *st saviour's church   york*
miscarriages   stillborn   brain fever or convulsions)
selina coughs from consumption   fourteen years left to live
'george make notes on provisions for passengers
weighs every day all supplies   water   bread   pork   beef
flour   counts   totals   squiggly figures fill his pages'

george – october
'spoke *scooner* from *africa*   either pirate or slaver
mr watson caught an albatross   seven feet wing tip to tip'
(killed without reason or mercy   george decides to stuff it)
rough seas   'hatches on women and children down all day'
fear coils round the heart like a rope noose tightening
'catherine morton is in irons and gagged in the poop
attempted to throw herself overbord but was caught by
robinson and sailor who left the wheel to save her'

george – november
'a great deal of lightening beautiful on the water
three albatross about saw a whale for first time
george sailor-boy flogged for being drunk
goodwin put in irons for given to him
taylor's child died   entered with full service'
travellers shiver freezing cold   'sea too rough to linger
mrs cavanah brought to bed of a son this morning
fine day   prayers in full'   twenty-two days later boy dies
squall takes down two sails and breaks boom
women grieve soundless screams   rock back and forth
drifting on the current   enter *bass strait* at daybreak
four months at sea   'john palmer dies after days of sickness
borne to the lee side of ship   union jack for a pall'

george – december 1841
daybreak see land   pass by *botany bay*
'scenery the most beautiful i ever saw'
fire off first gun   take on board pilot   fire second gun
'cast anchor all well' inspection by health surgeon
many small boats arrive to greet them
'at sea one one hundred and six days' logged in diary[23]
plus list of nails and lime   new ribbons and frock
'martin's child dies   buried it on shore'
george awarded salary four pounds

selina – december 1841
'george went on shore for first time
has employment with mr furton in *pitt street*
next day we take a house on *jamison lane*
fifteen shillings per week   pay one week in advance
boxes and ship-beds our only furniture
george counts in old testament and new
practice daily words and numbers improving his skill
books chapters verses for his diary   the 'word' occurs
six hundred thousand times and 'and' thirty-five hundred or more
patiently he dissects the bible   his hobby takes him years'

emma kershaw (1840–1841 december)
'daughter of george & selina kershaw died december 26th 1841
at *sydney* after lingering illness brought on by hunger and
starvation on board   *columbine* in her passage out from *england*
aged one year and three weeks and three days interred
in the *church of englan*d part of the cemetery at *sydney*'

george kershaw plasterer in *yorkshire*
columbine schoolmaster   could read   write and add
worked as plasterer on *government house*   *bridge street*
also *balmain*   moved to *braidwood* for selina's health
became police constable   contract builder
1878   died in *braidwood* and buried there

son william augustus kershaw in 1851
went to gold diggings in *bathurst* with george
(found £310 worth of gold)   became builders
(eureka! gold rush   violence   riots against *chinese*)
william m. isabella wilkinson had eight children
george wilkinson kershaw   m. matilda newton jermain
had nine children   my great-grandfather   rose specialist
1924   died in *wahroonga*   george w kershaw (eldest)
was nineteen when isabella died at thirty-six

born   married   + children   dies
marriage ring 'ribbon and frock'
women's stories buried with them
no contraception   babies pumped out like puppies
husbands urged offload sexual relief for good health

‘i bid you go fight for *white australia* in *france*’ billy hughes
  their destinies decided on battlefields of *europe*
  harold george augustus kershaw (1896–1968) (grandfather)
nurseryman at nineteen joined *anzacs* bound for *gallipoli*
later sent to *western front* given military medal for bravery
  champion rifleman fluent in *latin french arabic*
returned shell-shocked won the last *kings cup* rifle shooting
‘hg’ established *australia*’s first tree-seed supplier
  native seed collected distributed worldwide
1920 married frances mary king born *somerset england*
had two children girls helen and betty (my mother)
1968 ‘hg’ died *concord repatriation hospital*[24] *sydney*

  raymond newton kershaw (1898–1981) (granduncle)
1916 joined machine gun company *villers-bretonneux*
  disabled left arm pneumonia returns to *sydney uni*
1918 rhodes scholar *oxford* via *usa*[25]
1923 studied on scholarship at the *sorbonne*
  member of *league of nations secretariat*
1925 married hilda mary ruegg they had three children
1929 left *geneva* to join *bank of england*[26]
  awarded *companion of the order of st michael and st george*
met on trip to *sydney* ‘very model of a modern’ *english* banker
striped three-piece suit carried bowler hat and furled umbrella
who understood ‘equations both the simple and quadratical’[27]

after the wars

grandfather harold george kershaw (hg)
surrounded by jars of fine seed
dry   cold below house in my memory of him
colours gleam on glass   catch light
hessian bags line entrance
some filled with macadamia nuts
we would crack open with hammer
sit on stone dirt ground munching
izzy ran with his wheelbarrow
sorted   cleaned   dried native seed
spoke with hg who learnt arabic in palestine
who drove erratically yellow fj holden
on streets lined with flowering trees
to spot when ready for picking
granny was bookkeeper   telephonist
cranked black bakelite telephone
sorted mail   addressed small packets
sent all over the world
prized postage stamps return
washed   dry curling on sheets of newsprint
we played canasta determined to win
hg took me to hardware store   outside window
pushed my way to front of crowd
watched black and white images flicker
in a small square magic box

kershaw family, 1910: from left to right, raymond, edith, george, maude (in front) violet, hilda, matilda and harold (hg) (unknown photographer)

3

write now

journal

knock on door at 6 a.m.

'poverty is the worst form of violence' – mahatma gandhi

'please can you call triple 0?   need an ambulance   sorry'
see her distress   short satin robe   falling tears   bare feet
while phoning offer tea   'please milk two sugars haven't slept
in days went everywhere knocked on other doors no one would
open or slammed the door shut haven't eaten any chance
of bread and vegemite?'   on the sofa writhing in pain
swollen feet   weeping blisters   'never seen this before
think burnt meself in the shower cuz took me bag
no identity papers for *centrelink*   no tobacco   no tablets'
coughing 'no money'   make second cup   milk two sugar
heat wholegrain bun add butter vegemite   turn on tv
accident on *anzac bridge*   traffic chaos   hour passes
ambo arrives   she asks   'name   age   *aboriginal* or
torres strait islander?   '*aboriginal*'   'any illnesses?'
'diabetes' 'type one or two?'   'two'   'insulin or tablets?
when last did you have insulin?'   'four months maybe five'
takes glucose reading   '187 far too high   ulcers
infections   you risk coma   amputations'   stays calm
prepares saline drip   paramedic refuses to take to hospital
without someone to monitor her   'just put me in your truck
let me go with ya'   sobs   'sorry nobody opened their door
sorry please give me something for the pain been screaming
for days sorry no sleep pain too much'   given panadol
wait two hours for another ambulance to take her to hospital
clean away tissues cannula plastic bits rearrange my cushions

roadwork

1. tribes of the *gadigal* nation walk sacred country
   crows caw above well-worn track
leaves rustle underfoot   became dirt path
   1811 first toll road in the colony
horse and cart travellers link settlements
sydney cove (*warrane*) to *parramatta* (*burramatta*)
   hurry past *marcus clark* store now an emasculated *tafe*
stop-start   brake in rat-run congestion   honk horn
'planning' eight years later continues for *parramatta road*
   gentrification of the 'ugliest road corridor'
while westconnex mostly underground motorway booms
   'an urban transformation strategy'
confusing collection of roads become tollways
link at 'spaghetti intersection'   *rozelle* interchange
spilling out like pick up sticks remembered from childhood
cranes stretch necks to sky   a swinging skyline
   'wrong way go back' men in hard hats   yellow hi-vis
bottleneck *victoria road* trucking tonnes of dusty spoil
'infrastructure' shout hard-hat execs gleeful in photo-ops
declare open another short section to developers' tolls
saved laneway   add two kilometres of burning concrete
   (while with covid many workers work from home)
monster stacks to spew toxic breath deadly to humans
   picnic beside unventilated airshafts in green space

2. compulsory acquisition hundreds of homes
tunnel *homebush* to *haberfield* eight lanes under *newtown*
  include heritage houses in haberfield trees gone
malignant apartments metastasise in grey-white concrete
  mushroom upwards gaping holes appear gas leaks
roads close cracks spread across household walls
  little luck finding compensation for subsidence
sticky fingers are in public purse: social housing
  buses ferries flogged – it's a highway robbery
budget blowouts temperatures rise planet on the boil
(pm scott had pamphlet plan that relied on technological
advances while savage cuts defunded *csiro* and universities)
  indigenous poverty trauma entrenched by theft of country
poets painters music makers in economic exile
  university students can't afford higher fees debt
homeless women sleep rough spun into blankets

3. 1950s unfamiliar accents meld over food and coffee
buy wedding gowns cakes flowers hire photographer
  the past is shutting up shop 'for lease' businesses idle
council close iconic but dingy *olympia milk bar stanmore*
  no pot of tea or milkshake with art deco table service
brylcreemed and permed cheek-to-cheek couple in poster
who smile over retro counter faded chequered lino floor
in the dark an old man stranded in samuel beckett play
waits for his café to reopen into *blandesville*

4. concrete most widely used stuff on planet
   massive danger to human health
far more destructive to environment than plastic
   we drown in rivers of poured concrete
freeways become long row gardens while we build new highways
seoul and *mexico city* 'greening' theirs into verdant foliage
   (an oz plan did abandon concrete runway in *antarctic*)

disruption continues on fractured *parramatta road*
always 'on sale' *godfreys vacuum cleaners*   *costco*
fantastic furniture   *'hardly normal'*   *bob janes t-mart*
   bulldozed will 'make *sydney* great'   again?
roads spread snaky flashing red and silver along freeways
koalas bowled over by speeding trucks   wildlife retreat
future slums identical 'little' boxes stretch to treeless horizon
solo drivers whizz past rezoned car dealers' estates
   'going going gone'
'progress' grinds on out through this vast country   fast

what is old is new again

'either we go on as a civilisation or we don't' – greta thunberg

1. eighty years ago when *germany* invaded *poland*
tanks rattled into towns   soldiers rounded up civilians
books critical of regime burned   classical texts
fuelled fire   children wore yellow stars
taken by cattle trucks to death camps
   exodus of *jewish* refugees escaped by boat
to *palestine*   many were holocaust survivors
denied entry   *british* returned to camps in *germany*
sent back before creation of state of *israel* –
   settlers seize farms   destroy aged fig and olive trees
occupy stolen land   build homes   modern cities –
   palestinians denied citizenship   political suppression
under constant surveillance   indefinite incarceration
snipers shoot children who throw stones

born after world war two   live suburban life
find copy of *house of dolls*   holocaust porn
(*nazi* brothel *whores* in *joy division* have lesbian boss
who whips them) learn of 'illicit sex' from book
with photos of starved people in striped pyjamas
dead bodies   piles of shoes   hidden in linen cupboard
   with dad's .22 rifle   (a defence from possible
invasion by *reds* from the *north*) want to join *kibbutz*
plough in one hand   handgun in the other

2. bombsite cities of sand   homes crushed by giants
millions displaced seek shelter under canvas in camps
   on rising seas pour into rickety boats
small boy's body washed ashore on *turkish* beach
   photo splashed across world news
rescuers of migrants at risk in *mediterranean* face prison
south of border people flee countries *usa* helped destroy
among reeds and rubbish   drowned man
   infant daughter   float on *rio grande*
activists charged with transporting   harbouring
trafficking people   criminalised for giving water
   migrants dying in the desert
president trump calls press freedom 'enemy of the people'
journalism   'fake news'   émigrés 'animals'   'criminals'
'drug dealers'   'rapists'   immigration place in solitary
   homosexuals   disabled   mentally ill
forty days sixty thousand children held in squalid camps
kept caged   without family   hungry with no hot meals
   showers   unwashed clothes   lights always on
   some sexually assaulted   ill and dying
manacled mothers give birth   deported   babies left behind
witness democracy bought by scratch my back deals
   racism and lies   rise of *neo-nazi* thugs
who share *swastika*-cupcakes and online hate

3. strangled cry of white cockatoo overhead
sunny autumn morning in *sydney*
unseasonably warm   dead leaves rustle underfoot
driest continent on earth   dying towns
toxic rivers clogged with floating dead fish
  'climate emergency'   'water is gold'
  sold to highest bidder
water grab   cotton   to mining leases
new wars fought will be for control of water
  burning coal from *galilee basin*
pollution time bomb for our planet
  pm morrison portrays *manus* detainees
'murderers'   'child molesters'   'rapists'
  we have history of venal cruelty
convicts banished to *port arthur*   *norfolk island*
aboriginals to *cape barren* and missions
  most asylum seekers arrive by plane
  eighty-one thousand in four years
after 'miracle   how good is *austraya*' election
  loss of hope in offshore camps
  'seven years is enough   it's too much'
in one month forty-seven refugees attempt suicide
  seventy self-harm
border force sends asylum seeker boats back

orderly queue

we have forgotten history   world war two
footage of allied skeletal soldiers in rags
marching single-file shouts   brutal beatings
  jewish citizens   smuggled out of ghettos
escape long lines in concentration camps
taken to sea   find asylum   settle   raise family

seven hundred thousand *rohingya* on skyline
  form ragged queue   cross border
behind them   villages burn   smoke clouds skies
blood soaks grass   tents overflow on muddy ground
deals made with brutal regimes   costly border force
stop the boats those asylum seekers who don't drown
'jumped queue at sea'   held hostage as deterrent
  detained for years   kept prisoner in *png*

hands on heads   men on *manus* form orderly queue
march to transit buses   pet dogs beaten to death
thrown from bus window   fear locals with machetes
  arrested   handcuffed   some dragged   kicking
beaten with long metal poles   forcibly moved
  their futures undefined

remembering tiananmen square

people's liberation army in casual clothes
assemble in *great hall of the people*
change into uniform   'just obeying orders'
special forces clear every tent   power turned off
crackle of gunfire   flashes shatter the dark
soldiers slash burn thirty-three foot papier mâché
   statue: *goddess of democracy*
overhead helicopters throb   birds of prey circle
avenue of eternal peace   army tanks mobilise
   before assault   country boy
lies about his age   joins the army
given camera   twenty rolls of film
told to mingle with pro-democracy protesters
he keeps back three rolls
   tank-man in white shirt clutches shopping bags
matador with artillery tanks   holds the line
returns home with shaking hands prepares dinner
   escapes into exile or was he killed?
bbc news: 'ten thousand die in and around the square'
army photographer position smiles while soldiers pose
   inspired from his hidden rolls of film
that chen guang liao kept he paints
washed-out melancholy blues   on canvas
swirls of grey smoke rising   blood splatter graffiti walls
burning barrels   troops picking through rubbish
torn banners   scattered textbooks   broken bodies

tanks mash the dead stacked among mangled bicycles
bulldozers push crushed corpses into pits to burn
   1989   *australia*   bob hawke's tears fell
wept when read transcripts of massacre   a war crime
offered asylum forty-two thousand *chinese* students
ruled that none would be forced to return
   we are quarry for booming *chinese* economy
2021 *hong kong* police arrest organiser of vigils
   discussion or remembrance banned in *china*
social media stays blocked as punishments continue
dissidents   students   political prisoners   petty criminals
members of banned spiritual group *falun gong*
denied food   water   sleep   women raped
tortured with electric prods   flesh burnt
   tibetan monasteries remain in ruins
abandoned prayer flags flutter on *himalayan* hills
religion banned   displays of dalai lama's photo
considered separatism   'protesters' imprisoned
   million *uyghurs* from *xinjiang province*
interred in concentration work camps
forced to eat pork   drink alcohol   brutalised
'they crawl on all fours treated as less than dogs'
   china cannot hide genocide
spokesman says '*anti-china* forces set up to spread lies'
xi jinping 'nations that bully face bloodied broken heads'
meanwhile *china* accused of malicious hack-attack
state-sponsored criminals stealing intellectual cyber property

we who believe in freedom cannot rest

breaths – sweet honey in the rock

1. amerika

policeman's knee on throat eight minutes forty-six seconds
george floyd murdered on tv for all to see   *i can't breathe*
streets fill with peaceful protesters   some take the knee
enough is enough   agitators throw bricks   loot   burn stores
black lives matter   journalists blinded by rubber bullets
free press denigrated 'the enemy' purveyor of 'fake news'
cops walking past elderly man bleeding from head wound
toss him aside as if litter   man towers over young black girl
she doesn't flinch   holds his gaze   fists clenched   he yells
'fuck black lives matter   fuck you' police shoot eight times
breonna taylor killed in her home   searching for people
already in custody no drugs found   man in wheelchair
homeless bleeding   cop shot him with rubber bullets
man jogging   chased   hunted   executed   gun culture
how many deaths go unrecorded unseen   not investigated?
crisis of deaths in custody   true scope remains unknown
angela davis on police violence   'takes us way back to the
days of slavery   aftermath of slavery   development of
ku klux klan'   *no justice no peace   silence = violence*
who police the police?   when looting starts shooting starts
trump calls out national guard   mobilises the military
people pepper-sprayed clearing square for bible photo op

2. australia

'if we don't look at the past we can't craft the future' – linda burney mp

british occupy country name *terra nullius* or 'nobody's land'
aboriginals shot on sight poisoned chained put in leg irons
elders trucked over red earth like cattle to reservations
since 1991 end of royal commission into deaths in custody
four hundred sixty deaths no convictions
most incarcerated people on earth stolen generation
they took the children away[28] still happening today
forced removal hundreds of children ripped from families
six riot police forcibly restrain david dungay eating crackers
twelve times cried 'i can't breathe' dies in custody
yamatji woman joyce clarke shot dead by policeman
kumanjayi walker shot by *nt* policeman three times
boys tear-gassed *detention centre darwin* found 'unlawful'
australian rallies *no pride in genocide* prosecute police
tone-deaf politician calls protests 'selfish self-indulgent'
pm morrison against 'importing things happening overseas'
ignore climate science destroy environment mining rules!
rio tinto during reconciliation week blew up *juukan gorge*
sacred site from before ice age forty-six thousand years
continual occupation linked to present-day custodians
pm albanese government commits to a voice to parliament
indigenous recognition in constitution calls for referendum
white australia has a black history
always was always will be aboriginal land

yesterday's news

twenty-eight people die in fires firies perish
  two thousand and fifty homes lost
greedy politicians make promises they won't keep
to reduce emissions can find no common ground
drought-hit farmers given loans   mining company mates
tax-free 'incentives' never need refund   sold water
fracking   drilling contaminates precious drinking water
strip-mining seabed   sludge destroys ecosystems
rising sea levels sink low-lying *pacific nations*
great barrier reef whitened in warming acidic seas
overfishing   ocean fish stocks fall   fish flap-flop
in dirt puddles on dry riverbeds   rainforests burn
estimate fires kill 'five hundred million mammals
reptiles birds'   burrowing crawly creatures face extinction
whales gobble plastic   their bloated bodies beach on sand
bats and birds no longer fly   drop dead from on high
list goes on   air full of smoke and poison particles
flames finger ancient trees where koalas grasp the sky
pm cancels plans fly overseas promoting coal exports
  why in these burning times are fears and anger false?
'ravings of inner city loonies'   'bloody disgrace talk now'
  worldwide on fridays   children take to the streets
save our future   fight climate change or die frying

on conspiracy bandwagon

we will fight in face masks   gloves   gowns
disinfectant wipes   we will never surrender   this plague
this unseen enemy   batten down   close the borders
send back the cruise ships   there is talk of war
(could cancel purchase of just one nuclear submarine
or airplane   create free masks and sanitiser for all)
anti-vaxers mount attacks against restrictions
covid-19 is fake news?   a conspiracy?   9/11 hoax
virus manufactured in *china* or by *usa* lab?
  'world run by alien lizard people   drain the swamp'
  'buy survivors blood'   'over-reaction' hurts economy
  'bill gates vaccine can control cellular communications
  via 5g with the aim of killing millions   torch the towers'
facebook warns ninety million misinformation posts
australian government announce covid-19 modelling
  now swanning about on catwalk near you
czech republic nudists required to wear facemasks
magical thinkers have a god that will heal the chosen
  take you to heavenly rapture if prayer fails
a lonely busker sings 'we'll meet again' to absent crowd
  wild animals invade empty city squares   stay home
solitary healing   see light of clear skies   hear birdsong
breathe clean air not pollution   pause   plan   prepare
not for the future past but for new beginnings

just saying

women murdered in homes
on streets   in parks
night after night
just another day of slaughter
men taught hatred is ok
torture porn on tv
violence rips into bodies
torn rag dolls cast-off as worthless

start by naming shaming
words become weapons
'bitch' 'dyke' 'witch' 'cunt' 'terf'
  use as erasers
scorn smothers dissent
contempt flays skin
heavy blows rain down
on *aboriginal* women   blackout time
we just won't talk about it

'women support patriarchy'
who oppose *their* use of ladies' loo
'i am a woman'   rainbow hair   beard
hirsute arms   cock under frock – silencing sisters
  lack of privacy   triggering rape unease
dangerous ideas seen on *abc* breakfast news

roadblocks to recovery were signposts on the way

at fifteen   leave school   dental assistant *macquarie street*
printed out pamphlets   distributed   abortion law reform
seventeen left nursing *rpah*   shamed discovery nurse-lover
nineteen   road accident smashed leg   two years healing
years *drama school*   slight work ingénue scarred with limp
invalid years   time of mental illness   drugs   alcohol
friends die of aids   when revolution still seemed possible
play stages theatrical / political   anti-war *happening*
tour on rambling bus   *queensland* countryside
perform high schools   comedy   drama   poetry
adelaide act in ustinov play *halfway up the tree*
study black theatre at *flinders* stoned on too much lsd
then threw my life away   time came to stop
'wife' took another lover   young student whom she taught
she said 'stay'   borrowed airfare   left without delay
retreat to bushland   water surround rocks eagles sky soar
admission to *psych centre*   pills   weed mixed with booze
move back to *sydney* meet poets   brown burns and viidikas
   write   publish words   to excite   overthrow
with s.u.d.s act in the *crucible* and *bartholomew fair*
poverty and pain seven years in *darlinghurst* squat
glitter queens danced as mirror ball spun out-of-control
wrote fuming page-spatters express simmering rage within
years later sober-clean   live alone in rooms of my own
'world held in mind in life of a tree' or flight of birds

legacy

doomsday clock ticks closer to midnight
on horizon nuclear catastrophe
during last cold war *americans*
tested nuclear bombs in *marshall islands*
  thousand times bigger
than bombs they dropped on *japan*

soldiers pick by hand clumps of plutonium
  bury with tonnes of nuclear waste
on remote *runit* a porous coral atoll
under dome islanders call the *tomb*
that's cracking seawater splashes
  storm surges flood
plutonium leaks from beneath concrete blocks
  radiation oozes into blue lagoon
spreads across *pacific paradise*

rising sea levels drown sparkling slivers of land
  every high tide
women sweep radiated seawater from their floors

collateral damage

trump orders withdrawal of *american* troops that are buffer
between bashar al-assad and erdogan protecting *kurds*
hevrin khalef   senior feminist *kurdish* politician
secretary-general of *future syria party*
that believes in pluralism and equal rights for women
in democratic home to millions of *kurds*
betrayed by trump who left them to the wolves   war crime
soon forgotten   six years work undone in six days

barrage of bullets head riddled with gunshot wounds
some close range   shots to the back   face fractures
hit repeatedly with the butt of rifle   both legs broken
dragged by hair until it parted with her scalp
executed at checkpoint in *syria* by *jihadist* mercenaries
prisoners of war released by *turks* to fight in *syria*
former *isis* fighters who believe women inferior to men
shouting 'film me film me' they shoot already dead bodies
turkey claim vehicle struck by *syrian air force*
sensationalist *italians* report raped and stoned to death
fake news to further debase clever and gentle woman
turks broadcast   'khalef neutralised   success'

*

three years later: a women's revolution across *iran*
morality police kill kurdish-iranian woman mahsa amini
demonstrators defy hijab laws   chant 'woman   life   freedom'
give women a voice   our bodies are our own
   whether or not we bear children
activist zahra sedighi-hamadani sentenced to death
targeted speaking out to end persecutuoon lgbtqia+ in *iran*

spread of another virus

government grant for security alarms
cameras lights guard *horizon church*
where pm holds happy-clappy hand on high
government grant one hundred thousand dollars
aid *aboriginals* funds allegedly spent on staff admin

'hell awaits you repent only jesus saves'
  declares footballer from *tonga*
pentecostal preacher disperses messages on instagram
islanders in skirts 'warriors for jesus' 'god's police'
the new missionaries in the *kimberley*
'the prophetess' calls traditional beliefs 'devil-worship'
  sacred culture 'witchcraft from the devil'
brings to christ her dump-you-in-the-river
conversions of most vulnerable
'slain in the spirit' parishioners
speak in tongues collapse in religious ecstasy
on bonfires in remote communities
  throw ancestor artefacts into flames

praise freedom of religion
  that must be protected
'lifestyle violations won't be tolerated'

in pieces and pots

doctors pumped her head
full of electricity
without anaesthetic
when demons came
wait in line at seventeen
knowing what lay ahead
my mother   gentle   artistic
teenager won prizes for her drawings
published in newspapers married young
family's aim was for her 'to settle down'
two children before age of twenty-one
to escape control of drunk bully
retreated further when demons won

her ceramic biscuit barrel vase from pottery factory
in *museum of applied arts and sciences*
vases   dishes   ramekins and ashtrays
some hand-painted with *indigenous* art motifs
small round white plastic framed dried flower
arrangements sold to *david jones*
cheap imports and copies from *japan*
flood market   bankrupt in '60s   sell off stock
ceramic dutch boy and girl salt-and-pepper shakers
sold door to door mentioned in parliament
an outrage in *canberra* apparently

towards the end drawings and unfinished paintings
scattered in scrunched lumps on the carpet
turned toward the wall
still she laughs has lady in from next door
share few cold beers walks the block
exercises in municipal pool
continues to visit hospital for 'little rest'
respite from depressive swings and mania
medicated as nurses fuss enjoys her time 'away'

for years my mother wrote weekly letters
enclosed small money orders
sums hidden from 'the old man'
encouraged me to stay alive
'things will get better soon'

after she died received four ramekins
her hand-painted stolen *aboriginal* art
stylised stick figure blacks with spears
boomerangs kangaroo emu and goanna
anger and grief so overwhelm
smash them to pieces

’50s suburban mums and dads bought *australiana* ceramics to collect connect with outback often displayed behind glass in wooden cabinets *nixon (jemba)* sold directly to stores competed with martin boyd pottery both featured stylized *indigenous* subjects   plagiarism that infuriated me after smashing ramekins made some amends   two small vases from ebay as memories surface feel her presence when holding them remember her paintbrush   small swish of colour as storylines appear

https://collection.maas.museum/object/320006
earthenware vase by nixon pottery

nixon pottery (amends)

testing times

1. cannot stay must go home now fight the flight
old sandstone unfamiliar high-rise buildings offices
operating theatres 'packer's pecker' at *barangaroo*
shivering waves of freezing air conditioning
loneliness as buzzers *beep* machines ping outside
nurses' loud chatter inside panic mind-cycling
head miles loss of control fear don't overthink
  'call ambulance' doctor said low iron / blood loss
  swooning like 19th-century courtesan into bookcase
think flying fish rising on silver wings above waves

recall poet jan harry prisoner of her body in hospice
dying with dignity and grace dictating poems
spits grape skin in my hand bedclothes too smooth
  'try to get some sleep' says nurse breezy am too cold
think covid stalking corridors and conspiracy theories
lizard conspiracy theory where they rule the world
donated freezing blood transfusion to my veins
turning warm-blooded woman into lizard complain
nurse breezy 'no it's dragon blood' brings blanket
wind tunnel blasts ice storm as he closes door

behind mask someone's grandmother mother sister
wearily daily clean ward-world with mop and bucket
'tonight go home have shower put feet up rest do nothing
tomorrow cleaning go shopping do cooking go cemetery'

2. outside my door   elderly man seeks sobriety
   race-caller to god   shares prayers
   'right to go   wanna make the grade
we are off and ruining dear lord
skyrocketing sales first through barrier
leeches lead pack round the bend   on outside
comes *temptation*   followed by *degradation*
ice pushes through closely followed by *bottled insanity*
whiskey's breath to *bags of green*   further back
it's a dog's life   on the straight   *seduction* picking up
inside is *drug-free*   can he make it?   *on the nod* falls back
clean and sober takes lead suddenly defeats *enticed*
yay   gets up for the win   hallelujah
   well done   hallelujah   amen'
at least think that's what he said

on *ladies ward*   warrior women who snore
stubborn woman with very loud tv for five hours
nods off   snoring guns blazing   from next bed
'turn it down or i'll come over and bloody turn it off'
next day young 'mouthy' woman told she has cancer
   'how did old injuries happen   so many broken bones?'
husband's violence 'you are a no-good-for-nothing   ugly
sad loser'   she climbed over 4th-floor balcony   jumped
lifetime of pain   mouth a line of bitter resistance
'i don't take shit from no one' glares turns on tv   loud

3. as junior nurse after scrubbing bedpans toddled along
main hallway where white-veiled army sisters flew
wing-flapping long corridors pulled over as untidy
wet uniform began every morning inspections by matron
sent wood-panelled room head of board directors to explain
lesbian affair in nursing quarters both were outed separated
career-ending shame and ridicule left rpah memories burn

beat of steady rain wind gusts in frangipani leaves
sleep in my own bed room to paint view to die for
play music drown out women's screams drunk men
want to go jump in puddle news but not on *facebook*
witness cover-up young woman's rape in *parliament* office
crown casino to lose licence for alleged money laundering
myanmar aung san suu kyi wins election coup d'état
arrested by *junta* back in detention on trial again
nasa's *perseverance* lands on *mars* snow as *texas* freezes
ted cruz family forced to flee to holiday in sunny *cancun*
just as our pm did holidaying in *hawaii* during bushfires
'don't hold a hose mate and don't sit in a control room'
he backs gas-led economic recovery response to pandemic
beneath waves fins propel flying-fish to soar
high above rough seas flying free

a dance

as though climbing *mount everest*
pulls at bannister one step at a time
friends with everyone   loyal to none
voice in head accuses   'you hold me back
could be someone by now' partner clings to his arm
push on together toward impending avalanche
her blonde wig askew   too thin for the frock
as if at school formal leans for support from her beau
she's doing slow soft-shoe shuffle with 'jack dancer'
can she take her super early for the casket and plot?
rather buy himself a boat   dreams dissolve into debt
he steals her pills   stoned on *endone* and *methadone*
spends nights cleaning   scrubbing away
smells and stains of her disease
helps shake out his fears   failing her
in their cosy cocoon they squabble and squawk
like rainbow lorikeets looking for lice
her ashes in heavy box from funeral parlour
'she is the love of my life' he sobs
though not for long   money's gone
drugs to numb the pain and booze
says he's over it now   doesn't need sex
spinning out of control until the music stops

in the dark

holding hot coffee   walking stick   cannot see aisle
seat number   stumble   lights off
lit only by screen   ad blasts out fast car manoeuvres
   sit awkwardly   bump coffee cup   down thigh
hot coffee spills   drop f-bomb and again as heat burns
'fuuuck!' soggy upset having lost the lot 'geeze louise!'
   woman sits behind me   rips open packet of crisps
grinds her teeth   crumples   chews   begins to crunch
gulp   crackle   swallow another bite   gobbles down
family-size kettle sea-salt original chips   smell of grease
chippies scrunched through *sometimes always never*
stylish film that requires concentration
   deadpan *scrabble*-obsessed tailor searches for lost son
words pour like honey   stick to board   yet unable
express grief   gulps words like the woman chomps chips
pushes them down   turn to my friend   mutter 'what tha?
family-size crisps in a cinema!'   behind me spits chips
'at least don't swear'   would like to skin   slice   dice
boil   mash   roast or fry   burn her to a crisp
instead   say nothing

the underworld queens

kate leigh and matilda (*tilly*) devine
tough gangsters in skirts   decked out in silver fox furs
broad-brimmed hats   flash diamond rings
sydney's queens of crime   frocks as sharp as razors
   tilly's 'queen of the loo' deals cocaine   owns brothels
sp bookmaking   *chinese* opium dens in *woolloomooloo*
palmer street   *darlinghurst*   known as *razorhurst*
(cut-throat razor-gangs slicin' and dicin' the competition)
   tilly's lookin' after business at '*the bloodhouse*'
tradesman's arms   sawdust on the floor
soaks up all the blood and vomit
   kate's down at courthouse peeling vegies for tea
sly-grogger   fence for stolen goods   cocaine pusher
bookmaker   *queen of surry hills*   married petty crim
gave false alibi for 'shiner' the boyfriend
   does five-year stint for perjury   runs sly grog
standover men   slashers and enforcers
'go on' knock on the door   ask 'is mum in?'
cockatoos keep nit (watch) 'stay 'ave yer drinks inside'
   it's kate and tilly's *sydney*   they own the joint
rivalry fuels razor wars   frank green's shot over a girl
   ('good looker for a whore') armed pistols and knives
kate's mob arrives   *big jim* on tilly's porch
shoots one dead   wounds two or three more
kate's lover collects a bullet   razor gang turns streets red

kate kills *snowy* prendergast aged twenty-three
charged with murder   pleads self-defence
coroner records finding of shooting justified
prendergast 'burglariously' entered premises
women are rich   write letters to editor
interviews in the press   accuse each other
   'white slaver!'   'dope pusher!'
give generous gifts to charity
christmas parties for local kiddies
bribes to police   until '54 that is
   when taxman came
takes all their money   diamonds and property
penniless kate dies after stroke and fall
in upstairs room on *devonshire street*
seven hundred attend her funeral
crims and cops   well-known identities
even tilly devine pays respects
   (just to be certain)

tilly wrote to the *truth* newspaper
'wasn't as bad as was painted
there's lots in *sydney* who'll miss me
even coppers'   they soon forgot her
story goes in a pub in *darlinghurst*
someone proposed to raise a glass
toast her passing but no one bothered

rescue

when my cat of nineteen years died
  lucky heard there was a vacancy
last owner when drunk swore at neighbours
bellowed sad songs enough to scare screeching cat
drop-kicked and hurt not treated right
his cries drowning out waning moon
lucky could not listen to my music play
he'd prowl and growl would not stay
  an enigma dressed in fur my rescue tabby
looks out at views relaxed safe on windowsill
on my lap while country *emmy lou* sings she's blue
snuggles far from stale tobacco smell of beer
  purrs for soothing pats strokes under soft chin
lives out his slow days grows old and deaf
meditates in fugue state though appetite strong
  (pâté for puss with sauce ooze from the centre
luxury he lickety-laps) but still he howls
hold him tight sometimes yell
  company through *covid* isolation
in this it is he who rescued me

a dog's tale

post on facebook has story of a dog
beagle   lost in *kentucky* forest
who wanders round in circles
barking on woodland path
first marks birch   then red maple
oak-hickory again   fallen leaves rustle
afraid   hears call   'here dog   come here dog'
found   taken to animal shelter
put on 'kill list'   appears doomed
until beagle rescue group in *canada*
hear his plight   dog lovers' drive relay of hourly shifts
almost thousand kilometres from *kentucky* to *toronto*
woman working temporarily there   observes beagle
up for adoption   takes him home   calls the dog   guy

american actress   meghan markle
who marries prince harry   before wedding day
guy   lost dog from *kentucky*   (so story goes)
rides to be with his duchess at *windsor castle*
in backseat of range rover driven by her majesty
queen elizabeth II   queen of the *united kingdom*
as the saying goes 'every dog has its day'

lucy lorikeet

'there are openings in our lives of which we know nothing' – Jane Hirshfield, *The Envoy*

flightless   stunted wings   no tail feathers   'runner'
born with highly contagious beak and feather disease
baby rainbow lorikeet carried to my flat from garden
soft blue head   red eyes   her calm appraisal
                                        already at home
in the time of covid   we all are in cages   many die
  aged folk in nursing homes carried forth in body bags
lucy feeds formula to her friends mirror   bell   toy
bobs on perch hangs upside down whistles cage to rooms
                                        my replies echo from bedroom
taught her 'sexist' whistle like a labourer
                                        at 'piece of skirt' walking by
climbs walls of her cage   swinging   sometimes falls
bathes in small plastic bowl   shaped blue cat face
intense red yellow chest   purple blue belly   shades of green
                                        small single yellow tail feather
through worst of covid   two years and more
                                        we spend time together   companions
cheerful soul began to hide   head to droop   green diarrhoea
   bacterial infection took little bobbing   happy girl away
painting now   long swooping green wings
                                        tail feathers that touch the stars
                                        in glorious flight   she's ascending
                                        gold dust in her wake

coming down

icy winds bring down branches laden with snow
white magic thickly spread on ground
cold bites his skin   breath floats in air
smacks gloves together   thoughts stilled
as frozen lake   early morning *qigong*
smooth and calming   kitchen tidied
everything in its place   leaving *katoomba*
in the 'quiet' carriage   watching young man
eat crunchy cereal   scrape plastic container
lid *clicks* with resounding *snap*
layer of milk settles on lips   sprinkling of snowflakes
he's remembering empty white sheets
his lover's absence
a man reads *sydney morning herald*
rustling his newspaper   unfolds and carefully refolds
woman blows nose into tissues   soon three people
sniffling   snuffling   sneezing
slowly train rocks along tracks   almost yells
'enough this is supposed to be the quiet carriage!'
sun risen by time he reaches destination
appears shrunken in woollen overcoat
sweaty with too many layers of warm itchy clothing
exhausted   pushes his way through busy turnstiles
into clamour of yet another day in a city office

response to 'at the poetry reading' – john brehm

'i can't keep my eyes off the poet's wife's legs…' – poetry foundation

poet's wife sits restless uncrossing her legs
sighs   wishes husband read the room better
taxman's life could have mustered some laughs
his tedious childhood innocence   hay barns posies
thinks audience minds like hers are elsewhere
defrost the fridge / take cat to vet for desexing
this audience almost asleep except for *larry the lech*
eyes bulge licks at his lips   dribbles of spittle
trousers too small   tight round crotch that's bursting
poet reads *the lightest element* on hydrogen
wife hopes someone open a window and let oxygen in
sighs again   thinking of charlie's visit last night
poet in next room   she smiles   they had to be so quiet
lips on lips   wet   sweet breath and her clever hands

dark desire (after Carter Brown)

('60s pulp fiction writer)

saxophonist plays rainy night blues
man watches blonde with curves in all the right places
toss back vodka shots   tall   when she walks
bum wriggles with rhythm and bounce
dame for bad days   when drink
lines of white powder   fail to make life bearable
she looks trouble   he sidles over
          'buy you a drink honey'?
          'bugger off cowboy'
he moves casually to toilet   snorts 'white lady' courage
returns to find her with another hot babe
adjusts trousers   suddenly tight
          'wanna a drink ladies my shout'?
blonde frowns   'come on lover this place too crowded'
he looks around suddenly sees that all the women are in pairs
          'it's a bloody dyke bar'
feeling shame   follows the women out
hollow footsteps in laneway   up ahead the women laugh
he increases his pace   abruptly   tall woman turns
          'you following us'   feet apart   'ya looking for trouble'?
he can't see a problem   shrugs   'come on girls can't we party'?
attempts to grab her but quick lunge and man is left holding
aching genitals wishing he'd just stayed home
          'my amazon!' whispers lover

thread

on phone with gay male friend
reading politician's online post   she complains
  'cannot abide women who would by word or deed
disempower any woman within her circle
  that those so-called *feminists* do more damage
to our mothers   sisters   daughters   acquaintances
than almost anything or anyone else'   wow   more than rape
or murder?   or by rude gesture   texts   clowning around
offend by alleged groping grabbing buttocks   breasts
women branded liars   troublemakers silenced as less than
  performance to maintain safety is exhausting
  wear camouflage weaponize keys carry pepper spray
  cover drink   avoid eye contact   don't walk alone at night
attempt to clarify   share thoughts
  in my opinion *feminism* is belief in and advocacy of women
  that opposes *patriarchal* systems but not men themselves
while watch on tv president trump   sexual predator
  orange clown   spout sanctimonious sound bites
am struggling to get word in over the phone
  where another unequal power play unfolds
rolling commentary on wonder of beautiful young man
who stokes flames of desire and 'so smart' trading quips
flattered by my elderly-wealthy-white friend's teasing *wit*
who coyly asks down the line 'well what else could it be?'

golden girl (betty cuthbert 1938–2017)

awkward in flowery frock
served tea   sandwiches   cake
on gran's best rose-patterned china
ten when i met her
celebration for 'golden girl'
who won three gold medals
blonde curls   sunny smile
see her on black and white tv
sprint   mouth open   win
women laugh in the kitchen
futures filled of possibilities
book of 1956 *melbourne olympics*
green cover   golden torch with red flame
all cuthberts' sign   rose growers
nurserymen like my great-grandfather
horticulturalists like my grandfather
since 1969 the champion has multiple sclerosis
forty-eight years in wheelchair   limbs wasted
going nowhere fast   faith keeps her strong
tireless advocate   sells 'betty cuthbert' roses
fundraising for cure   blooms golden at the heart

words in passing (les murray 1938–2019)

last time i saw him   glasses perched on tip of nose
striped yellow and red woolly jumper
cap pulled down   a smile lingered on his lips

pot of thick porridge bubbling on the woodstove?
smell of bush smoke   blackened billy
perhaps gone with cattle in early morning dew
   green grass   poddy-calf's forlorn calls
or poet from *bunyah* reads by fireside flames
   les murray born in *nabiac* as my father was
went to same school though years apart
   said he still used an old typewriter
couldn't trust computers feared striking wrong key
   find himself on a porn site   police in riot gear
guns drawn   instantly break down his door
  love sound of typewriter in the morning
swish   clickety-clatter of keys   poems flow free
mastery of words summoned by fast flying fingers

les told he could not find or buy himself new typewriter
might search internet but for that would need computer
wrote his son had found him one   'a new/old portable
   with ribbons ordered from *london*   my fingers relish
springiness of keys after long depravation'

poem for vicki (vicki viidikas 1948–1998)

her pen knocked down wankers
like bowling ball would tenpins
woman in gypsy scarf with wicked smile
she sipped tea from cracked rose-china cup
at breakfast fed bits of burnt bacon
to butch the cat who drooled 'ribbons of pearls'

vicki left school at fifteen   abuse-survivor
gave me copy of *condition red*
inscribed 'your mad lovely laugh'
poems of grace and intensity
fiery words that cascaded to paper
cackled and crackled   lightning strikes hissed
words to inflame   to set a cat among the pigeons
she had notebooks for unpublished novel set in *india*
i typed chapter *kali and the dung beetle*
read *cuttack* (*orissa*) from 'india ink' at the *nimrod*
she scathed purchase of nuclear weapons and warships
while filthy children played in sewerage by *ganges*
that now fills with covid-19 bodies floating down
from *uttar pradesh* and are netted

nothing private anymore when tide goes out
round fire-eye glimpsed in pavement puddles
love-messenger journeys across stone skies
take me back to the good times

silence

from the distance two *chinese* spy ships observe
talisman sabre fire live ammo on *great barrier reef*
   as coral bones bleach white in warming seas
russians test unstoppable hypersonic nuclear missiles
we'll protect nations borders but what of the planet?
   after twenty years in dusty boots and camouflage fatigues
shambolic exodus as people fall from sky above *kabul*
afghan army evaporates back to their villages
handmaidens in black again walk with male chaperones
   war looms in *europe*   repeat cycles of blood for profit
after last shot fired   hear silence of the dead
give way to birdsong   killing grounds no more
become green pasture   flowering fields of grain
while 'dick race' to space billionaires play tourist guide
those that the war on poverty missed sleep rough
   on rain-soaked sheets of plastic or in cars
woman pushes pram carrying supplies to *newtown* park
strapped in tubs of vegetarian food bag of apples
homeless women with children in pelting sudden downpour
take shelter under trees   in toilet block   wait   damp   hungry
wait for food   lacking shelter   refuge bed   (they're closed)
pandemic stalks streets in stranger's cough or sneeze
white birds flutter on breeze   do bomb-makers go to a park
admire nest-building skills   plan to bomb all to smithereens?

dear francine at the factory

words of wisdom recollect how she calls it prose-poety running words that stutter then flow together form rivers drawing thoughts feelings places people ordinary like me into poems that underneath have undertow draw you in and under in rip-rifts that open out or drown she said healing comes from shared experience good to wash out put on the line let ink dry have lost plot again whole chapters lost under covers squashed into bed listening to jeanne lewis sing *razon de vivir* (reason to live) hair gone grey feeling useless dumped like old books to landfill outside woman yells to her dogs 'come back' bolted like my thoughts feverish anger anxiety returns some scars are worn on the outside proudly like tattoos some secrets buried so deep they're almost forgotten yet linger long after injury scratch 'em they'll bleed filling forms at hospital past illnesses operations list grows battle scars arrogance strutted as strength ignorance as virtue heroin addict kicked me in the face left a long white line 'you are complex' nurse informs 'focus slow down' wars lost few victories before gift of sobriety life lived body well-used before recycling

recollections

said he'd rent me a room mattress on floor depression drags my heels don't paint whitewashed walls 'gunna but' drink too much make loud racket hear him late at night banging on typewriter words of wonder he travels to *india* i move to squats – butterfly i'm pinning you down not on a hedged-bet hook but in my bitterness book oh you'll fly away again become unstuck but i've stopped mothering you now with luck– (arrogance powers a dog in drink) winter chills derelict life years later sober scrubbed clean (sobriety: healing bruised and battered soul so often traumatised as a child) meet again we talk of books and loss anguish from a woman's scorn early lovers his desire for pretty young men (i ask can we discuss the weather instead) win two tickets *nsw art gallery garden and cosmos indian summer life in royal court of the maharajah of jodhpur* (he'd visited palace in *rajasthan*) energy bursts 'jitterbug raving' concubines delight him so many exquisite women dancing across canvas people say no one is bisexual they just can't choose but he deeply loved all beauty contagious ecstasy and passion his bed a hive of books confined to hospice ganesh on wall buddha catholic cross covers all bets on the afterlife (his larrikin grin 'that is all fiction anyway') feel the loss rigour of his mind sardonic humour kindness sifting words he so understood obsessive need to keep writing

shoot

miss lily magnolia from the deep south

'big game huntin' so expensive since rhinoceros elephant tigers became endangered trump brothers are wild don jnr shot elephant cut off tail as a trophy legends they're true conservationists if all tha' wildlife goes there's nothin' left to shoot big business breedin' lions on 'canned farms' eight thousand of 'em only twelve hundred left in the wild hand-reared cubs taken for pettin' zoos they're so easy to shoot 'cos they're so tame in the *savannah* get close to lioness ya can almost see her blink shots fired bam thud thrillin' rich hobby hunters use bow and arrows sometimes they miss giraffe not that difficult high-powered rifle does tha' job porters arrange her all neat folded up like starched linen napkin careful camera duddent miss tha' shot you draped over dead giraffe put it up on wall alongside mounted animals ya killed leopard antelope big red kangaroo at top-dollar tourist park join a shooter's outback adventure package hunt farmed big reds or emus (ya can't hunt 'roo in *oz* not like in *texas*) tha' reminders of tha' cuddly soft toys ya had as a child: purple elephant green lion striped pink giraffe y'all it shure is fun'

gratitude

at nearly eighty hammers into submission music hasn't played since a boy beethoven's 'moonlight sonata' on hundred year old baby grand in aged care hostel 'this arrangement is very tricky sorry if i make a mistake i'll start over' worry we could be here all night as he fluffs another chord says 'perfection is at the horizon we are here now' we laugh woman next to me plays keys on back of her hand smiles with pleasure as the music swells remarks 'how lovely' sadly traps both hands between her thighs embarrassed stops tapping he became a friend gave me hope advice on my poetry catcher of errant apostrophes charming often cantankerous english teacher in *papua new guinea* poetry editor with *overland* sick drank too much had black eye when climbed the steps in early eighties to 'meetings meetings meetings' four years later i followed up the same steps memories become faded scars (active addiction to booze or drugs is to be tossed in a machine set on slow-wash buffeted by a sudden deluge in dramas and disasters with no money) he thought in rehab *catholics* had him when he read writing on the wall in gothic script 'grant me the courage to change the things i can' now *catholics* have him again he has his own small bedroom bathroom balcony plants paintings desk laden with mementos help choose *thai* silk shirt applause as power of music to heal resonates 'a success!' miracle is we stay sober drink tea eat cake smile despite everything

riches from white ho of the west

found junk mail that came in my inbox toxic masculinity see him now at computer typing with one finger his plan for riches from the *west*

'think before you do somethink your actions may have unpleasant effect how would truly feel whenever all your family members or friends witness you take proper care of yourself i have poisoned selected adult internet sites using virus that steal all files from your system obtains access to cameras and lots more so today have film of you doing your stuff clip of you wanked in modified video to fit tv screen so will be a lot more exciting everyone to enjoy anyways if you need me to remove all contacts with movie five hundred sum i need in crypto-currency to leave you on your own completely (*address supplied*) you can quickly find details on web how you can use this payment method if you have no clue this email has invisible tracking tool inside i will be aware when you going to check from that moment on you will be given two days make up your mind if perhaps for whotever reason i don't obtain my money i promise that each and every contact from your list will see this video you welcome to get in touch with your local cops or whotever really doubt can help'

opened few times no message from contacts yet though have never visited porn site or had photos taken of my nether region (boobs dropping on saggy tum over depleted bush) no pictures to share but could be someone's grandma – disgraceful!

space tourists

'cartoonish space dick' giggled tv talk show host richest man in the world jeff bezos blasted off in *blue origin* ten-minute all-inclusive flight on *new shepard* float free in zero gravity *amazon* magnate behemoth bookseller return from space stetson cowboy pays under 1% in tax thanks his customers workers who can't unionise have unsafe work conditions heard must piss in a bottle to save time wasted on toilet visits 'you guys paid for it' great phallus penetrated blue skies on suborbital journey *glans penis* floated to earth by parachute petition called bezos be denied re-entry alleged he is 'lex luther evil overlord hell-bent on global domination' beaten by virgin's branson in billionaire 'show ya mine' vanity space-race project or is this an 'end of term high school science contest?' tourism and colonisation to plunder planets trash outer space like earth? i prefer to bicycle not rocket science see that earth warming extreme weather events *western europe* drowning *china* flooding (worst in thousand years) wild fires ice caps melting seven hundred million people below poverty line in pandemic weatherman 'in not too distant past only rich could afford to travel by train we all go now will be same with space travel extreme downpours due in *sydney* floods up north'

times they change

twas dark and windy night when woken by sounds unusual driven out to investigate from the safety of bed   a crash and boom   back gate swung open rustling clucking shrieks from the hen house soon follow   shadow falls from out the dark gives me this night a fright   takes leap to bring him down right thin fella   no meat on these bones all right
deals for mining mates and military done as virus of poverty spread thru land soon stun   infamy   unemployed on the move seek jobs where they're none
'just wanted few eggs to feed my family   chook came running pecks at my throat   had knife   sliced to save my life'
'i've lost my head   where are we going?   cannot see what's ahead   neck in a bucket   like *hills hoist* round in circles my feet run   play me no sad songs   king rooster   old cock-boiler is dead   no respect   gone'
told rowdy don't you show your face in this chook pen again gave him carcass   few eggs to take home   apology to mr bob dylan but this twas: *murder most fowl*

heavy-handed?

wants to bring his cousin   his cousin's offsider   to help get my speakers connected and vacuum cleaner to clean back of tv and amplifier   he asks that i leave men to work as had distracted him day before with my chatter and anxiety   he then assures me he knows what he's doing   i can trust him   over and over tells me that he loves me   worked for famous man   wired up all his electrical stuff   names him   should go have cuppa with friend or to my room   he's already told me not to touch anything as there could be live wires and i'd be harmed   electrocuted even   as an older lesbian living with disabilities am getting fearful   have lost my wifi   hours of calls with telstra   thought better move the box to where it's easier to see   said he'd been in 'gunnawannacouldaland' before   cousin will know what to do   boxes   bits and bobs strewn through two rooms left there from day before   wiring coiled in anticipation 'you wanted us to come before six' 'no' i said 'just not after nine'   all the while being managed as 'the little woman'   why didn't he say he just didn't know instead of 'well this is the easy bit now' in an attempt to set up wiring   'did you blow them speakers up maybe? do you really need them? look these speakers maybe great but soundbar better' 'nah' i said to him 'not having three blokes and a vacuum cleaner in my house' gave him fifty dollars calls me 'mad old chook'   poet friend says i'm a 'badass warrior queen'   somewhere in between i can be found waving my walking stick at the sky   'mate i'll make other arrangements ok' nbn service-man found what my neighbour did   'completely unfathomable'   he really didn't have a clue at all

stay safe

covid-19 has burst the bubble floats freely in *sydney* feeling unsafe in 'letdown' / lockdown? locked away in vaccination 'stroll-out' against *delta variants / omicron* (not name of new band) but virulent disease that has antivaxers at rallies chanting 'lockdowns infringe our rights' 'free-*dumb*!' (they punch police horses don't they?) in pandemic spreading virus they don't believe real but worldwide conspiracy or the flu scary times as numbers rise not reassured that only those unvaxxed or with underlying conditions risk death try to bunker down escape economic recovery *zoom far aparties* with avatar friends play *monopoly* launch poetry books be a landlady of the future socially forage internet-universe invest in digital real estate buy virtual properties tour your small plot in simulated neighbourhoods hold art photo fashion or video displays as derivatives of the real world buy or sell at nine hundred thousand crypto and rising millionaires or small investors (domains start at ten dollars ninety-five) search metaverses in mirror world of collective virtual reality interact with others in computer generated environmental space travel to holiday safely from home without actually leaving this how it ends staring at a screen paralysed with hope?

brittney griner

‘don’t let my life end here’   tears fall   pleas ignored
nine years in brutal *russian* prison   hustled out of court
two times olympic *american* basketball gold medallist
205.74 cm (six foot nine)   men's shoe size seventeen
star centre   icon of the game   plays during off-season
(rumoured for a million dollars)   *russian* premier league
(in *usa* men paid two hundred times more than women)
   sniffer dog found hash-oil in two vape cartridges
had doctor’s script for pain   she packed without thought
found in bag at airport   last seen wearing black hoodie
proclaimed ‘black lives for peace’   long locks dangle free
   (you can be charged in *russia* for holding in protest
blank piece of paper)   power games in play
fierce advocate for lgbt rights   her frame squashed
too big for van taking to and from court   hands cuffed
towers over guards   already held six months   pleads guilty
‘there was no intent   didn’t want to break the law’
she wrote ‘without protection of my wife   family friends
terrified might be here forever’   a *kremlin* pawn?
   she’s everything that putin’s toxic masculinity fears
black   beautiful   champion athlete   gentle woman has wife
   arrested less than week before *russia* invaded *ukraine*
neither *russia* or *usa* want to be seen as too sympathetic
   religious right do have powerful hold on both
prisoner swap talks   *kremlin* warns ‘no megaphone diplomacy’
month later   hundreds of thousands military conscripts
drafted to fight in *ukraine*   resistance met with brutal repression

postscript (after all is said and done)

ukraine

1. is this how the world ends
'not with a bang or a whimper'
nuclear blast in an illegal land grab
that annihilates the human race?
    takes courage to leave   a hero to stay
  brother against brother   peace talks fail
russia under financial siege while *ukraine* blown apart
days after putin said he wanted to 'de-nazify' democracy
tv tower hit   metres from *babyn yar holocaust memorial*
(genocide by bullets   thirty-four thousand jews massacred
marched to deep ravine   *german* soldiers shot in two days)
putin's war against 'degenerate degradation attitudes' (*lgbtqi+*)
he's just another 'cook in the kitchen of politics' (antigone)
  threats of chemical warfare biological weapons
the aged   women   children   shelter underground
when sirens stop   witness catastrophic destruction
no water   no food   no power   bombardment continues
five million refugees+   some freeze to death at the border
donations of weapons from *nato* pour into *ukraine*
skies fill with snow   rain   *russian* aircraft blitzing cities
maternity hospital hit   pregnant   face cut by flying glass
dressed in polka-dot pyjamas   teddy bear t-shirt
disorientated gives birth to girl women are dehumanised
raped as trophies of war   (easier to murder)
  mud bogs down *russian* tanks on road to *kyiv*

missiles target refugees   deadly attack at train station
message scrawled in *russian* 'for the children'
moscow crowds courageously chant no to war
   called 'scum   traitors'   face years in prison
john lennon + yoko ono's bed-ins against *vietnam* war
singing   'all we are saying is give peace a chance'
three hundred-fifty *european* radio stations
private and public broadcast the song against invasion
seven oligarchs suspicious deaths   *mariupol* falls *odessa* next?
russians launch obliteration *eastern front* in battle of *donbas*

ukraine a crime scene   'atrocious banality'   war drags on
propaganda   fake news   actors play their parts?
winter is coming   gas supplies bombed
footage show villages with no homes left intact
reduced to rubble   looted apartment blocks
people survive in cellars   mandatory evacuations
muddy craters   booby trapped bodies   hell
did *russians* bomb pow camp? kill heroes of *mariupol*?
no *russian* guards harmed   cover up war crimes?
torture genital mutilation   summary executions
slaughter of thousands   civilians buried in mass graves
   don't want to write a shopping list of disasters
missiles bombs rockets   where silence can't be trusted
russians fire missiles use the nuclear power plant as shield
'one miscalculation away from nuclear annihilation'

lismore nsw australia (it's not the same but…)

2. imagine losing everything you own
held precious   escaping with your life unrelenting rain
homes flooded to ceilings   residents drown holding on
older women still in nighties carried to safety
children hold dogs chest-high tight through water to safety
native animals die   cattle drown   trees uprooted by high winds
topsoil stains water red   flushed down rising rivers
ses volunteers   a community in small boats save lives
residents and shopkeepers return to stinking toxic mould
mud army with brooms and spades pull people's lives apart
piled up on pavements   ruined stock and furniture stacked high
electricity outages   sewage spills   landslides
airdrops to isolated communities as army called in
war zone   no food   no power   no phone   no pm (missing again)
huge waves batter beaches that now are unrecognisable
death toll rises
   lives washed away   flood refugees
people who cut   punched through roofs
suffer without homes   tradies in short supply
restoration takes time   mental health healing
unable to cook   camping out inside muddy homes
lismore left to rescue itself   scammers rip off residents
in shadow of trauma   there's more rain on the way
sceptics of climate change drowned out by heavy rain
extreme temperatures soar in the *antarctic* as sea ice falls
reports are of *covid* cases rising with peak yet to come

a grifter at my door

'her death brings great sadness'
king charles speaks as the new monarch
of his mother's service and commitment to duty
her funeral on all channels   great pomp and pageantry
until coffin lowered as her piper played final lament

three-thirty am   new neighbour next door   an older woman
cleans path back and forth   straw broom gathers debris
six am   feeding screeching seagulls and pigeons
singing joy unpacks boxes   raw hacking cough fills cold air
thin   no teeth   in her nightie   almost before drawing breath
on my doorstep with empty cup for milk
'been homeless for six years   fifty-four days
your place is so lovely gran   looks like a museum
me cheque doesn't come till thursday'
give her carton of milk   cough lollies   ten dollars
tide her over   know what it's like living cheque to cheque
three hours later she returns asking for more

first nations people grapple with mixed emotions
'sorry business without end'   during queen's visit on a tour
fences were erected to cover with branches
yorta yorta[29] people hidden from view

Notes

1. arrival and departures

1. group of indigenous people whose traditional lands are located in gadigal on eora country current location of sydney nsw australia
2. aboriginal name for sydney cove
3. https://www.sbs.com.au/news/the-feed/did-you-know-there-were-12-africans-on-the-first-fleet
4. https://sydneylivingmuseums.com.au/convict-sydney/convicts-colony
5. captain arthur phillip, commander of first fleet
6. a bunch of damned whores – lyrics, ted egan
7. john hunter, *an historical journal of the transactions of port jackson and norfolk island*, john shopdale, london, 1793, p. 70
8. https://sydneylivingmuseums.com.au/convict-sydney/convicts-colony
9. https://www.mq.edu.au/macquarie-archive/lema/about.html lachlan & elizabeth macquarie archive
10. governors' despatches to and from england, historical records of australia, australia
11. *australian dictionary of biography*, volume 2, mup, 1967: rose, thomas (1754–1833) by arthur mcmartin
12. https://www.geni.com/people/thomas-rose-snr-free-ettler-bellona
13. https://sydneylivingmuseums.com.au/convict-sydney/convicts-colony
14. generic term for aboriginal dance
15. mitchell library nsw, https://www.wikitree.com/wiki/rose-226
16. *australian dictionary of biography*, volume 2, mup, 1967: rose, thomas (1754–1833) by arthur mcmartin

17. dyarubbin (hawkesbury river) a beautiful and haunting place
18. photo rose cottage kathy green 2020
19. https://www.mq.edu.au/macquarie-archive/lema/about.html lachlan & elizabeth macquarie archive
20. https://australianroyalty.net.au/individual… henry buttsworth
21. family history research by ms wilga nixon (aunt)

2. another voyage

22. kershaw diary
23. gwen burchell & daughter nola, who digitalised george's diary
24. marjorie perry, harold george augustus kershaw, lance-sergeant
25. penny ferguson, *ben and his mates*, echo books, 2018
26. james cotton, raymond kershaw (1898–1981)
27. 'i am the very model', d'oyly carte opera co, john pryce-jones

3. write now

28. song, archie roach, member of the stolen generation, proud gunditjmara and bundjalung man – rest in the dreamtime
29. traditional *yorta yorta* lands lie on both sides of the murray river roughly from cohuna to albury/wodonga.

www.ingramcontent.com/pod-product-compliance
Lightning Source LLC
Chambersburg PA
CBHW070311120526
44590CB00017B/2623
* 9 7 8 1 7 6 1 0 9 4 3 1 6 *